50 Bread Recipes from Around the World

By: Kelly Johnson

Table of Contents

- Baguette (France)
- Ciabatta (Italy)
- Focaccia (Italy)
- Sourdough (USA/Europe)
- Brioche (France)
- Pumpernickel (Germany)
- Rye Bread (Scandinavia)
- Challah (Jewish)
- Naan (India)
- Roti (India)
- Paratha (India)
- Lavash (Armenia)
- Injera (Ethiopia)
- Pita (Middle East)
- Arepa (Colombia/Venezuela)
- Cornbread (USA)
- Soda Bread (Ireland)
- Bannock (Scotland/Canada)
- Pretzel (Germany)
- Panettone (Italy)
- Stollen (Germany)
- Tsoureki (Greece)
- Kulich (Russia)
- Babka (Jewish/Eastern Europe)
- Simit (Turkey)
- Bolillo (Mexico)
- Concha (Mexico)
- Marraqueta (Chile)
- Hokkaido Milk Bread (Japan)
- Melonpan (Japan)
- Baozi (China)
- Mantou (China)
- Pandesal (Philippines)
- Cuban Bread (Cuba)
- Anpan (Japan)

- Butterkuchen (Germany)
- Scone (UK)
- Johnny Cake (Caribbean)
- Tortilla (Mexico)
- Fougasse (France)
- Lángos (Hungary)
- Tiger Bread (Netherlands)
- Crumpet (UK)
- Bagel (Jewish/Poland)
- Dampfnudel (Germany)
- Lefse (Norway)
- Pogacha (Balkans)
- Obwarzanek Krakowski (Poland)
- Banneton Bread (France)
- Cuban Medianoche Bread (Cuba)

Baguette (France)

Ingredients:

- 3 ½ cups (440g) bread flour
- 1 ½ teaspoons salt
- 1 ¼ teaspoons instant yeast
- 1 ¼ cups (300ml) warm water

Instructions:

1. Mix flour, yeast, and salt, then add water. Knead for 10 minutes until smooth.
2. Cover and let rise for 1 ½ hours.
3. Divide into 3 pieces, shape into baguettes, and let rise for 45 minutes.
4. Preheat oven to 475°F (245°C) with a pan of water inside.
5. Slash tops and bake for 20-25 minutes.

Ciabatta (Italy)

Ingredients:

- 4 cups (500g) bread flour
- 1 ½ teaspoons salt
- 1 teaspoon instant yeast
- 1 ½ cups (360ml) water
- 2 tablespoons olive oil

Instructions:

1. Mix flour, yeast, salt, water, and oil. Knead until sticky and smooth.
2. Cover and let rise for 2 hours.
3. Shape into loaves and let rise for 45 minutes.
4. Bake at 425°F (220°C) for 25 minutes.

Focaccia (Italy)

Ingredients:

- 4 cups (500g) all-purpose flour
- 1 ½ teaspoons salt
- 2 teaspoons yeast
- 1 ½ cups (360ml) warm water
- ¼ cup (60ml) olive oil
- 1 tablespoon rosemary

Instructions:

1. Mix flour, yeast, and salt. Add water and oil, knead for 5 minutes.
2. Let rise for 1 ½ hours.
3. Press into a baking sheet, dimple the dough, and top with rosemary.
4. Bake at 400°F (200°C) for 20-25 minutes.

Sourdough (USA/Europe)

Ingredients:

- 4 cups (500g) bread flour
- 1 cup (240ml) sourdough starter
- 1 ½ teaspoons salt
- 1 ½ cups (360ml) water

Instructions:

1. Mix flour, starter, and water. Knead for 10 minutes.
2. Let rise for 4-6 hours. Shape into a round loaf and let rise overnight.
3. Bake at 450°F (230°C) for 40 minutes.

Brioche (France)

Ingredients:

- 3 ½ cups (440g) all-purpose flour
- ¼ cup (50g) sugar
- 1 teaspoon salt
- 1 packet (7g) yeast
- 4 eggs
- ½ cup (120ml) warm milk
- ½ cup (113g) butter, softened

Instructions:

1. Mix flour, sugar, salt, and yeast. Add eggs and milk, knead for 10 minutes.
2. Incorporate butter and knead again. Let rise for 2 hours.
3. Shape into a loaf, let rise for 1 hour.
4. Bake at 375°F (190°C) for 25-30 minutes.

Pumpernickel (Germany)

Ingredients:

- 2 cups (250g) rye flour
- 1 cup (125g) whole wheat flour
- 1 teaspoon salt
- 1 teaspoon instant yeast
- 1 ½ cups (360ml) warm water
- 2 tablespoons molasses

Instructions:

1. Mix flours, yeast, and salt. Stir in water and molasses. Knead until smooth.
2. Let rise for 2 hours.
3. Shape into a loaf, let rise for 45 minutes.
4. Bake at 375°F (190°C) for 40 minutes.

Rye Bread (Scandinavia)

Ingredients:

- 2 cups (250g) rye flour
- 2 cups (250g) bread flour
- 1 teaspoon salt
- 1 teaspoon caraway seeds
- 1 teaspoon yeast
- 1 ½ cups (360ml) warm water

Instructions:

1. Mix flours, yeast, salt, and seeds. Add water and knead for 10 minutes.
2. Let rise for 1 ½ hours.
3. Shape into a loaf, let rise for 45 minutes.
4. Bake at 375°F (190°C) for 35 minutes.

Challah (Jewish)

Ingredients:

- 4 cups (500g) bread flour
- ¼ cup (50g) sugar
- 1 teaspoon salt
- 1 packet (7g) yeast
- 2 eggs
- ½ cup (120ml) warm water
- ¼ cup (60ml) vegetable oil

Instructions:

1. Mix flour, yeast, sugar, and salt. Add eggs, oil, and water, knead for 10 minutes.
2. Let rise for 2 hours.
3. Divide into 3 pieces, braid, and let rise for 1 hour.
4. Bake at 375°F (190°C) for 30 minutes.

Naan (India)

Ingredients:

- 3 cups (375g) all-purpose flour
- 1 teaspoon sugar
- 1 teaspoon salt
- 1 teaspoon yeast
- ¾ cup (180ml) warm milk
- ¼ cup (60ml) yogurt
- 2 tablespoons melted butter

Instructions:

1. Mix flour, yeast, sugar, and salt. Add milk, yogurt, and butter. Knead for 10 minutes.
2. Let rise for 1 ½ hours.
3. Divide into balls, roll out, and cook on a hot skillet for 2 minutes per side.

Roti (India)

Ingredients:

- 2 cups (250g) whole wheat flour
- ½ teaspoon salt
- ¾ cup (180ml) warm water

Instructions:

1. Mix flour and salt. Add water gradually and knead for 10 minutes.
2. Let rest for 30 minutes.
3. Divide into balls, roll out, and cook on a hot skillet for 1 minute per side.

Paratha (India)

Ingredients:

- 2 cups (250g) whole wheat flour
- ½ teaspoon salt
- ¾ cup (180ml) warm water
- 2 tablespoons oil or ghee

Instructions:

1. Mix flour, salt, and water to form a dough. Knead for 10 minutes, then rest for 30 minutes.
2. Divide into balls, roll each into a circle, spread oil or ghee, fold, and roll again.
3. Cook on a hot skillet, flipping until golden brown.

Lavash (Armenia)

Ingredients:

- 3 cups (375g) all-purpose flour
- 1 teaspoon salt
- 1 teaspoon sugar
- 1 teaspoon yeast
- 1 cup (240ml) warm water

Instructions:

1. Mix flour, yeast, sugar, salt, and water. Knead for 10 minutes and let rise for 1 hour.
2. Divide into balls, roll into thin sheets, and bake at 450°F (230°C) for 3-5 minutes.

Injera (Ethiopia)

Ingredients:

- 2 cups (250g) teff flour
- ½ teaspoon salt
- 2 ½ cups (600ml) water
- ½ teaspoon baking powder

Instructions:

1. Mix teff flour, water, and salt. Let ferment overnight.
2. Stir in baking powder, then cook like a pancake in a skillet without flipping.

Pita (Middle East)

Ingredients:

- 3 cups (375g) all-purpose flour
- 1 teaspoon salt
- 1 teaspoon sugar
- 2 teaspoons yeast
- 1 cup (240ml) warm water

Instructions:

1. Mix flour, yeast, sugar, salt, and water. Knead for 10 minutes and let rise for 1 hour.
2. Divide into balls, roll into circles, and bake at 475°F (245°C) for 5 minutes.

Arepa (Colombia/Venezuela)

Ingredients:

- 2 cups (250g) pre-cooked cornmeal (masarepa)
- 1 teaspoon salt
- 1 ½ cups (360ml) warm water

Instructions:

1. Mix cornmeal, salt, and water into a dough. Rest for 10 minutes.
2. Shape into patties and cook on a skillet for 5 minutes per side.

Cornbread (USA)

Ingredients:

- 1 cup (120g) cornmeal
- 1 cup (125g) all-purpose flour
- 1 teaspoon baking powder
- ½ teaspoon salt
- 1 cup (240ml) milk
- 2 eggs
- ¼ cup (60ml) melted butter

Instructions:

1. Preheat oven to 375°F (190°C).
2. Mix dry ingredients, then stir in milk, eggs, and butter.
3. Bake for 25 minutes.

Soda Bread (Ireland)

Ingredients:

- 4 cups (500g) all-purpose flour
- 1 teaspoon baking soda
- 1 teaspoon salt
- 1 ½ cups (360ml) buttermilk

Instructions:

1. Preheat oven to 400°F (200°C).
2. Mix flour, baking soda, and salt, then stir in buttermilk.
3. Shape into a round loaf and bake for 40 minutes.

Bannock (Scotland/Canada)

Ingredients:

- 2 cups (250g) all-purpose flour
- 1 teaspoon baking powder
- ½ teaspoon salt
- ¾ cup (180ml) water

Instructions:

1. Mix flour, baking powder, salt, and water into a dough.
2. Shape into a round, flatten, and cook on a skillet for 5 minutes per side.

Pretzel (Germany)

Ingredients:

- 3 cups (375g) bread flour
- 1 teaspoon salt
- 1 teaspoon sugar
- 2 teaspoons yeast
- 1 cup (240ml) warm water

For boiling:

- 8 cups (2L) water
- ¼ cup (60g) baking soda

Instructions:

1. Mix flour, yeast, sugar, salt, and water. Knead for 10 minutes, then let rise for 1 hour.
2. Shape into pretzels.
3. Boil in baking soda water for 30 seconds, then bake at 450°F (230°C) for 15 minutes.

Panettone (Italy)

Ingredients:

- 4 cups (500g) bread flour
- ¼ cup (50g) sugar
- 1 teaspoon salt
- 2 teaspoons yeast
- 4 eggs
- ½ cup (120ml) warm milk
- ½ cup (113g) butter, softened
- ½ cup (75g) raisins
- ½ cup (75g) candied fruit

Instructions:

1. Mix flour, yeast, sugar, and salt. Add eggs and milk, knead for 10 minutes.
2. Knead in butter, then fold in raisins and candied fruit. Let rise for 2 hours.
3. Bake at 350°F (175°C) for 40 minutes.

Stollen (Germany)

Ingredients:

- 4 cups (500g) all-purpose flour
- ½ cup (100g) sugar
- 2 teaspoons yeast
- 1 teaspoon salt
- 1 teaspoon cinnamon
- ½ cup (120ml) warm milk
- 2 eggs
- ½ cup (113g) butter, softened
- 1 cup (150g) raisins
- ½ cup (75g) chopped almonds
- ½ cup (75g) candied citrus peel
- ½ cup (120g) marzipan (optional)

Instructions:

1. Mix flour, sugar, yeast, salt, and cinnamon. Stir in milk, eggs, and butter. Knead for 10 minutes.
2. Fold in raisins, almonds, and citrus peel. Let rise for 1 ½ hours.
3. Shape into a loaf, placing marzipan in the center if using. Let rise for 30 minutes.
4. Bake at 350°F (175°C) for 35-40 minutes. Dust with powdered sugar when cool.

Tsoureki (Greece)

Ingredients:

- 4 cups (500g) bread flour
- ½ cup (100g) sugar
- 1 teaspoon salt
- 2 teaspoons yeast
- ½ cup (120ml) warm milk
- 3 eggs
- ½ cup (113g) butter, melted
- 1 teaspoon orange zest
- 1 teaspoon mahleb (optional)

Instructions:

1. Mix flour, yeast, sugar, salt, and zest. Add milk, eggs, and butter. Knead for 10 minutes.
2. Let rise for 2 hours. Divide into three ropes, braid, and let rise for another hour.
3. Bake at 375°F (190°C) for 30-35 minutes.

Kulich (Russia)

Ingredients:

- 4 cups (500g) all-purpose flour
- ½ cup (100g) sugar
- 1 teaspoon salt
- 2 teaspoons yeast
- ½ cup (120ml) warm milk
- 3 eggs
- ½ cup (113g) butter, melted
- ½ cup (75g) raisins
- ½ cup (75g) candied fruit

Instructions:

1. Mix flour, yeast, sugar, and salt. Add milk, eggs, and butter. Knead for 10 minutes.
2. Fold in raisins and candied fruit. Let rise for 2 hours.
3. Shape into a tall pan and let rise for another hour.
4. Bake at 350°F (175°C) for 40 minutes.

Babka (Jewish/Eastern Europe)

Ingredients:

- 3 ½ cups (440g) all-purpose flour
- ½ cup (100g) sugar
- 2 teaspoons yeast
- ½ teaspoon salt
- ½ cup (120ml) warm milk
- 3 eggs
- ½ cup (113g) butter, softened

For the filling:

- ½ cup (100g) chocolate chips
- ¼ cup (50g) brown sugar
- 2 tablespoons cocoa powder

Instructions:

1. Mix flour, yeast, sugar, and salt. Add milk, eggs, and butter. Knead for 10 minutes.
2. Let rise for 2 hours. Roll out dough, spread with filling, and roll into a log.
3. Twist and place in a loaf pan. Let rise for 1 hour.
4. Bake at 350°F (175°C) for 35-40 minutes.

Simit (Turkey)

Ingredients:

- 3 cups (375g) all-purpose flour
- 1 teaspoon salt
- 2 teaspoons yeast
- 1 cup (240ml) warm water
- 2 tablespoons molasses
- ½ cup (75g) sesame seeds

Instructions:

1. Mix flour, yeast, salt, and water. Knead for 10 minutes.
2. Let rise for 1 hour. Divide into pieces, roll into ropes, and twist into circles.
3. Dip in molasses, then sesame seeds. Bake at 400°F (200°C) for 20 minutes.

Bolillo (Mexico)

Ingredients:

- 3 ½ cups (440g) bread flour
- 2 teaspoons salt
- 2 teaspoons yeast
- 1 ¼ cups (300ml) warm water
- 2 tablespoons vegetable oil

Instructions:

1. Mix flour, yeast, salt, water, and oil. Knead for 10 minutes.
2. Let rise for 1 ½ hours. Shape into ovals and let rise for another 30 minutes.
3. Slash the tops and bake at 400°F (200°C) for 25 minutes.

Concha (Mexico)

Ingredients:

- 4 cups (500g) all-purpose flour
- ½ cup (100g) sugar
- 1 teaspoon salt
- 2 teaspoons yeast
- ½ cup (120ml) warm milk
- 3 eggs
- ½ cup (113g) butter, softened

For the topping:

- ½ cup (113g) butter, softened
- 1 cup (120g) powdered sugar
- 1 cup (125g) flour
- 1 teaspoon vanilla or cocoa powder

Instructions:

1. Mix flour, yeast, sugar, salt, milk, eggs, and butter. Knead for 10 minutes.
2. Let rise for 2 hours. Divide into balls.
3. Mix topping ingredients, roll into discs, and place on top of dough.
4. Bake at 350°F (175°C) for 20-25 minutes.

Marraqueta (Chile)

Ingredients:

- 4 cups (500g) all-purpose flour
- 2 teaspoons salt
- 2 teaspoons yeast
- 1 ½ cups (360ml) warm water

Instructions:

1. Mix flour, yeast, salt, and water. Knead for 10 minutes.
2. Let rise for 2 hours. Divide into 4 pieces, shape into rolls, and let rise for 30 minutes.
3. Slash the tops and bake at 400°F (200°C) for 25 minutes.

Hokkaido Milk Bread (Japan)

Ingredients:

- 3 ½ cups (440g) bread flour
- ¼ cup (50g) sugar
- 1 teaspoon salt
- 1 tablespoon yeast
- ½ cup (120ml) warm milk
- 1 egg
- ¼ cup (60ml) heavy cream
- 2 tablespoons butter, softened

Instructions:

1. Mix flour, yeast, sugar, salt, milk, egg, and cream. Knead for 10 minutes.
2. Let rise for 1 ½ hours. Shape into a loaf, let rise for another hour.
3. Bake at 350°F (175°C) for 30 minutes.

Melonpan (Japan)

Ingredients:
For the bread:

- 3 cups (375g) bread flour
- ¼ cup (50g) sugar
- 1 teaspoon salt
- 2 teaspoons yeast
- ¾ cup (180ml) warm milk
- 2 tablespoons butter

For the topping:

- ½ cup (113g) butter
- ½ cup (100g) sugar
- 1 cup (125g) flour

Instructions:

1. Mix bread ingredients, knead for 10 minutes. Let rise for 1 hour.
2. Mix topping ingredients, roll into discs.
3. Shape dough into balls, cover with topping, and bake at 350°F (175°C) for 20 minutes.

Baozi (China) – Steamed Filled Buns

Ingredients:
For the dough:

- 3 ½ cups (440g) all-purpose flour
- 2 teaspoons yeast
- 2 tablespoons sugar
- 1 cup (240ml) warm water

For the filling:

- ½ pound (225g) ground pork
- 2 tablespoons soy sauce
- 1 tablespoon oyster sauce
- 1 teaspoon sesame oil
- 2 green onions, chopped

Instructions:

1. Mix flour, yeast, sugar, and water. Knead for 10 minutes. Let rise for 1 hour.
2. Mix filling ingredients.
3. Divide dough, flatten, fill, and seal. Let rise for 30 minutes.
4. Steam for 15 minutes.

Mantou (China) – Steamed Buns

Ingredients:

- 3 ½ cups (440g) all-purpose flour
- 2 teaspoons yeast
- 2 tablespoons sugar
- 1 cup (240ml) warm water

Instructions:

1. Mix ingredients and knead for 10 minutes. Let rise for 1 hour.
2. Roll into a log, cut into pieces, and let rise for 30 minutes.
3. Steam for 15 minutes.

Pandesal (Philippines)

Ingredients:

- 4 cups (500g) all-purpose flour
- 2 teaspoons yeast
- ¼ cup (50g) sugar
- 1 teaspoon salt
- 1 cup (240ml) warm milk
- ¼ cup (60ml) vegetable oil
- ½ cup (60g) breadcrumbs

Instructions:

1. Mix flour, yeast, sugar, salt, milk, and oil. Knead for 10 minutes.
2. Let rise for 1 ½ hours.
3. Shape into rolls, coat with breadcrumbs, and let rise for 30 minutes.
4. Bake at 350°F (175°C) for 20 minutes.

Cuban Bread (Cuba)

Ingredients:

- 4 cups (500g) bread flour
- 2 teaspoons salt
- 2 teaspoons yeast
- 1 tablespoon sugar
- 1 ½ cups (360ml) warm water

Instructions:

1. Mix flour, yeast, sugar, salt, and water. Knead for 10 minutes.
2. Let rise for 1 hour.
3. Shape into loaves, let rise for another hour.
4. Bake at 400°F (200°C) for 30 minutes.

Anpan (Japan) – Sweet Red Bean Bun

Ingredients:

For the dough:

- 3 ½ cups (440g) bread flour
- ¼ cup (50g) sugar
- 1 teaspoon salt
- 2 teaspoons yeast
- 1 cup (240ml) warm milk
- ¼ cup (60g) butter, softened

For the filling:

- 1 cup (250g) sweet red bean paste

Instructions:

1. Mix dough ingredients, knead for 10 minutes, let rise for 1 hour.
2. Divide dough, fill with red bean paste, and seal.
3. Let rise for 30 minutes. Bake at 350°F (175°C) for 15-18 minutes.

Butterkuchen (Germany) – Butter Cake

Ingredients:

- 3 cups (375g) all-purpose flour
- ½ cup (100g) sugar
- 2 teaspoons yeast
- 1 teaspoon salt
- ¾ cup (180ml) warm milk
- ¼ cup (60g) butter, softened

For the topping:

- ¼ cup (60g) butter, melted
- ¼ cup (50g) sugar
- ½ cup (60g) sliced almonds

Instructions:

1. Mix dough ingredients, knead for 10 minutes, let rise for 1 hour.
2. Press dough into a baking pan, brush with melted butter, and sprinkle sugar and almonds.
3. Bake at 375°F (190°C) for 20-25 minutes.

Scone (UK)

Ingredients:

- 2 cups (250g) all-purpose flour
- 2 teaspoons baking powder
- ½ teaspoon salt
- ¼ cup (50g) sugar
- ½ cup (113g) butter, cold and cubed
- ½ cup (120ml) milk
- 1 egg

Instructions:

1. Mix flour, baking powder, salt, and sugar. Cut in butter.
2. Stir in milk and egg.
3. Roll out dough, cut into circles, and bake at 400°F (200°C) for 15 minutes.

Johnny Cake (Caribbean)

Ingredients:

- 1 ½ cups (190g) cornmeal
- ½ cup (65g) all-purpose flour
- 1 teaspoon baking powder
- ½ teaspoon salt
- ½ cup (120ml) milk
- 2 tablespoons butter, melted

Instructions:

1. Mix dry ingredients, then stir in milk and butter.
2. Shape into small cakes and cook in a skillet for 3-4 minutes per side.

Tortilla (Mexico)

Ingredients:

- 2 cups (250g) masa harina
- ½ teaspoon salt
- 1 ¼ cups (300ml) warm water

Instructions:

1. Mix masa and salt, then slowly add water. Knead for 5 minutes.
2. Divide into balls, roll out, and cook on a hot skillet for 1-2 minutes per side.

Fougasse (France)

Ingredients:

- 3 ½ cups (440g) bread flour
- 2 teaspoons salt
- 2 teaspoons yeast
- 1 cup (240ml) warm water
- ¼ cup (60ml) olive oil

Instructions:

1. Mix ingredients and knead for 10 minutes. Let rise for 1 ½ hours.
2. Shape into an oval and cut slashes. Let rise for 30 minutes.
3. Bake at 400°F (200°C) for 20-25 minutes.

Lángos (Hungary) – Fried Bread

Ingredients:

- 3 cups (375g) all-purpose flour
- 2 teaspoons yeast
- 1 teaspoon salt
- ¾ cup (180ml) warm milk
- ½ cup (120ml) water
- Oil for frying

Instructions:

1. Mix flour, yeast, salt, milk, and water. Knead for 10 minutes, let rise for 1 hour.
2. Divide dough, stretch into discs, and fry in hot oil for 2 minutes per side.
3. Serve with sour cream and cheese.

Tiger Bread (Netherlands)

Ingredients:
For the dough:

- 4 cups (500g) bread flour
- 2 teaspoons salt
- 2 teaspoons yeast
- 1 ½ cups (360ml) warm water
- 2 tablespoons butter

For the topping:

- ½ cup (60g) rice flour
- ¼ cup (60ml) warm water
- 1 teaspoon sugar
- 1 teaspoon yeast

Instructions:

1. Mix dough ingredients, knead for 10 minutes, and let rise for 1 ½ hours.
2. Mix topping ingredients, let sit for 20 minutes.
3. Shape dough into a loaf, spread topping over it, and let rise for 30 minutes.
4. Bake at 400°F (200°C) for 25-30 minutes.

Crumpets (UK)

Ingredients:

- 2 cups (250g) all-purpose flour
- 1 teaspoon sugar
- 1 teaspoon salt
- 2 teaspoons yeast
- 1 ½ cups (360ml) warm milk
- ½ teaspoon baking soda

Instructions:

1. Mix flour, sugar, salt, yeast, and warm milk. Let rise for 1 hour.
2. Stir in baking soda.
3. Heat a griddle, place metal rings, pour batter, and cook for 5 minutes until bubbles form. Flip and cook for 1-2 minutes.

Bagel (Jewish/Poland)

Ingredients:

- 4 cups (500g) bread flour
- 2 teaspoons salt
- 1 tablespoon sugar
- 2 teaspoons yeast
- 1 ¼ cups (300ml) warm water

For boiling:

- 8 cups (2L) water
- 2 tablespoons honey

Instructions:

1. Mix flour, yeast, sugar, salt, and water. Knead for 10 minutes and let rise for 1 hour.
2. Shape into rings and let rise for 30 minutes.
3. Boil for 1 minute per side, then bake at 425°F (220°C) for 20 minutes.

Dampfnudel (Germany)

Ingredients:

- 3 cups (375g) all-purpose flour
- 1 teaspoon salt
- 2 teaspoons yeast
- ½ cup (120ml) warm milk
- 2 tablespoons sugar
- 2 tablespoons butter

For steaming:

- 1 cup (240ml) milk
- 2 tablespoons butter

Instructions:

1. Mix dough ingredients, knead for 10 minutes, and let rise for 1 hour.
2. Shape into rolls and let rise for another 30 minutes.
3. Heat milk and butter in a pan, place rolls inside, cover, and steam for 20 minutes.

Lefse (Norway)

Ingredients:

- 2 cups (450g) mashed potatoes
- 1 cup (125g) all-purpose flour
- ½ teaspoon salt
- 2 tablespoons butter, melted

Instructions:

1. Mix mashed potatoes, flour, salt, and butter into a dough.
2. Divide into balls, roll out thin, and cook on a hot griddle for 1-2 minutes per side.

Pogacha (Balkans)

Ingredients:

- 4 cups (500g) all-purpose flour
- 1 teaspoon salt
- 2 teaspoons yeast
- 1 cup (240ml) warm milk
- ¼ cup (60ml) olive oil

Instructions:

1. Mix flour, yeast, salt, milk, and oil. Knead for 10 minutes.
2. Let rise for 1 hour, shape into a round loaf, and let rise again for 30 minutes.
3. Bake at 375°F (190°C) for 35 minutes.

Obwarzanek Krakowski (Poland)

Ingredients:

- 4 cups (500g) bread flour
- 1 teaspoon salt
- 2 teaspoons yeast
- 1 cup (240ml) warm water

For boiling:

- 8 cups (2L) water
- 2 tablespoons honey

Instructions:

1. Mix flour, yeast, salt, and water. Knead for 10 minutes.
2. Let rise for 1 hour, shape into twisted rings, and let rise for another 30 minutes.
3. Boil for 30 seconds per side, then bake at 425°F (220°C) for 20 minutes.

Banneton Bread (France)

Ingredients:

- 4 cups (500g) bread flour
- 1 teaspoon salt
- 2 teaspoons yeast
- 1 ½ cups (360ml) warm water

Instructions:

1. Mix flour, yeast, salt, and water. Knead for 10 minutes.
2. Let rise for 2 hours in a banneton (proofing basket).
3. Bake at 450°F (230°C) for 35 minutes.

Cuban Medianoche Bread (Cuba)

Ingredients:

- 4 cups (500g) bread flour
- ¼ cup (50g) sugar
- 2 teaspoons yeast
- 1 teaspoon salt
- 1 cup (240ml) warm milk
- ¼ cup (60g) butter, melted

Instructions:

1. Mix flour, yeast, sugar, salt, milk, and butter. Knead for 10 minutes.
2. Let rise for 1 ½ hours.
3. Shape into rolls and let rise for 30 minutes.
4. Bake at 375°F (190°C) for 20 minutes.

www.ingramcontent.com/pod-product-compliance
Lightning Source LLC
LaVergne TN
LVHW061953070526
838199LV00060B/4098